I0756257

FINISHING LINE PRESS
www.finishinglinepress.com

Her Names, Her Wits

poems by

Danika Paige Myers

Finishing Line Press
Georgetown, Kentucky

I will be
swallowed in the cost of
putting footprints in the sand.

—Susan Howe, "Hinge Picture"

Her Names, Her Wits

For Signe Virgil Hurwitz

ISBN 979-8-89990-460-8 First Edition

ACKNOWLEDGMENTS

Grateful acknowledgment is made to the editors of NELLE for publishing an earlier version of "Alberton Road Hike to Ruins of Oella Mill and St. Stanislas Church."

I could never thank everyone who played a role in the creation of this manuscript, but I would particularly like to acknowledge the contributions of: its early readers: Amy Amoroso, Scott Weaver, Renee Angle, and Tiffany Vann Sprecher; the students in my Spring and Fall 2024 University Writing: Poetry + Research classes, who created writing exercises that led to first drafts of many of these poems; my parents, 10/10, would have raise me again; Seth and Signe, my two favorite people to visit a cemetery with; Grendel, joy of the household, most beloved of dogs; Jessica McCaughey, who texted me about the ghost of T. Rowe Price; and my many poetry teachers, including Jennifer Atkinson, Li-Young Lee, Eric Pankey, John Rosenwald, and especially Susan Tichy, who has always been so generous with her time and her encouragement.

Publisher: Leah Huete de Maines
Editor: Christen Kincaid
Cover Art: Danika Paige Myers
Author Photo: Danika Paige Myers
Cover Design: Elizabeth Maines McCleavy

Order online: www.finishinglinepress.com
also available on amazon.com

Author inquiries and mail orders:
Finishing Line Press
PO Box 1626
Georgetown, Kentucky 40324
USA

Contents

i. Taft Pioneer Cemetery

it's twenty nineteen
and it's beach week
in the back seat
my mother and I

double needling
the shade of the
coast road
into shawls

Fold Beam Fault
Bramble Bond Stilt

between us
my daughter begins
to weep

Gorse Leach Gore
Gates Grade Orange

she's three
why are you crying my sweet
her breath in heaves
you've never taken me

to a cemetery
my mother and I
make eye contact
we smile but
her face is serious

Horsey Order
Bellknap Power

it's a hotel on a cliff
above the sea
at check-in we ask
where's the nearest cemetery
improbably
the lady points
across the street
the *street* is *Highway 101*

in order to climb higher
we have to walk under

Rites Bloom
Rush Dooms

log trucks and RVs
rumble
over the tunnel

my dad goes
OH OH OH
and it echoes

Established in 1906
nine acres of land
generously donated
by Mr. John Bones

above the sea
spring heath
white and purple
sweet peas
horned seablite
grey stones
and stone seats

Strange Gross
Rude Cross

I never want to leave
this place and
it's a cemetery so
maybe you can have that wish

my parents sit on a bench
looking out at the waves
while we three sound out
the names on the graves

Downy Round Moore
Flood Grass Hoard

ii. Northern Lights

it's twenty fifteen
I'm about to have a baby
and my mother
has brought me a quilt

the stars in their unspoiled night skies   the heavy
suns of harvest time images of a ship's compass
David's crown   a field of stars in a flag

each pieced star
made from dark fabric
covered in stars
your father and I were married for seven years
and didn't have any children
then we moved to Alaska and I had
two babies in two years
I told him we have to get out of this state
on the back the Northern Lights
are bands of saturated greens and blues
stitched over the dark
by my mother's hands

Mash Nails Kern
Back Roles Stern

we hang it next to the bed
sometimes I flip up the corner
and run my finger over the place
where my mother
stitched her name

Wells Carter
Lantern Miner

Druid Ridge
used to be
Annandale and before that
the tribes of the Piscataways
called that bit of land—

there are names
that aren't written
anywhere

Neptune
Horn Moon

textiles left on display
wear away

old quilts may have been made into saddle blankets covers for a chicken coop a dog bed hung over the opening of the outhouse or barn in place of a door placed on the floor or repurposed as batting for a new quilt

what can you learn
when all you have left
is the weight

of a scrap stitched
under a new plot
of squares and triangles

Jump Tall
North Starr

iii. Druid Ridge Cemetery

it's twenty twenty
and it's spring
when I start to run
in the cemetery
every morning

Hedgepeth Fisher
Spindle Spencer

names
from graves
make rhymes
my brain saves

Knight Watch
White Hatch

little chants
that match
my pace

cemeteries
have four functions
the hygienic function
places for sorrow
contact with eternity and—

when I see a friend's name
on a gravestone
I don't snap a photo
and send it to her

Drain Hare Soop
Round Chase Loop

iv. Ceremony for Burial of the Dead

it's twenty nineteen
my daughter, four, calls her
great aunt *Fifi*
tells Fifi *I love mummies*
and I also want to be
a mummy When Fifi
tells her *oh no!*
you don't want to be
a mummy she clarifies
yes when I'm dead I want
to have my organs put in jars
and then they'll put salt
on my body and wrap it up
and I'll be a mummy

I give her long
strips of linen
selvedge edges
I cut away
from legs and pockets
for new pants

Dates Dial
Strong Winder

she wraps
her American
Girl Doll
carefully from
her feet
covers her face

when the wrapped
doll is laid in the pink
plastic crib

she begins to fill
plastic Easter
eggs with ceremonial
objects gold Mardi
Gras beads

barbie shoes a tiny
quilt my mother pieced
a green skull ring

Starling Flower Chance
Ironmonger Stance

v. Macleay Road and Druid Ridge Cemetery

it's two thousand nine
my new husband's
last name officially
appended to mine
on the marriage
certificate

my grandmother
met him
didn't live
to see me wed him

Blessings Storms Gold
Lamp Hood Lord

as we drive out of state
instead of stopping
at Willamette National
Cemetery where
the fresh grave
marker reads *Virgil*
*Elizabeth Myer*s we make
a pilgrimage
her house is for sale
but not yet sold

in the back yard
we pick all
the raspberries
left on the canes
it's June
our vows are new
green pint boxes
in the cooler
berries like jewels

Bland Grub
Fair Herb

at every dusty
gas station and
national park

parking lot I sneak
the cooler
open place
one or two
on my tongue
squash them

If I tried to speak
I would cry they are
so cold and sweet

Robin Hobb
Sheckells Gill
Berry Lodge

it's twenty twenty-one
and cicadas dry new wings
in the sun *simply to*
the cross I cling goes
a stone saint
with a cicada clinging
between her toes

the smell of cicada meat
rotting inside
a million carapaces
crunching under our feet
the dog's tongue lolling
from gobbling
up the dead

Swan Fox
Locke Cog

some of the names
on the graves are words
and some seem like words
because they make
sounds you've
heard sketch
the skeleton
of our neighborhood

Buckingham Forbes
Hopkins Hawthorne

there's *Ralston* there's
Purvis elbowing into *Waldron*
the granite graves turn
silver in the shade
shade the pale grey
of granite drapes
from Midvale to Pinebrae
Smiths give way to *Slades*

we brush away cicadas
to make a purple crayon
rubbing of the grave
that says NOT DEAD
BUT SLEEPING

Marsh Stoke
Heath Pole Coke

vi. Mending

it's twenty twenty
we're making do

some mends
spend little
time and earn
new life
for old cloth

Vermillion Pelt
Wisdom Belt

holes moths stole
away filled
with new
yarn pilled
fabric shaved
a sweater saved

there's no wear
there below the left
shoulder
that's a hole
that was eaten
darn it and it won't be back

Nettles Hook
Brewer Hack

But where
the cloth thins
because
your body bends
it bends it bends
it slowly, slowly thins it
—these are places where
there's no good way to mend it.

Gilded Bower
Bankman Power

The fabric bad
clear up the arm
the thigh you stretched
this stretched it
this thigh
is a sigh away
from shredding

the cemeteries of the city
the most frustrating
open spaces
for developers

fringe belt
development
desire for profit
allotted to a cemetery
not matched by a contemporary
desire to remove existing burial grounds

you can try
to darn a patch
but where you've bent
and bent
the denim thin
a single stitch
might twitch
apart the fiber twist
that latticed thread
to cloth

Cuss Crisp
Hose Bliss

vii. Clotho (Holding Scissors)

I can believe in spinning

the substance of a life
twines chain-plied
back on itself

it's twenty twenty again
and my daughter
has training wheels
on her bicycle it's hard
to pedal up the incline
between Elmwood

and Maple Slope
and not made
easier by the potholes

Basil Buck
Heretick

we go around we double back
we go around
a sound
the ground we found
we double back
attack
keep track

Freeman Hill
Goober Peck

we twist
take risks
go frisk

By chain plying you know
that there will be virtually no
wasted singles

find bones
lose homes

Grace Bacon Lane
Chambers Major Drake

begin again
every inch of spun
singles has been turned
into a finished yarn

we mourn what's lost
we pay the cost

we're blind we've fought
we've bought the
plot or lined
our coats with coins

Cobb Watts
Show Alt

one fate is great
another knots

I'm always trying to get the maximum amount of yarn out
of my most precious and expensive fiber

it's just a twist
of thoughts
wound round
the sounds
of names and knots

Wink Young
Cable Tongue

we turn around
we're flying down
delight and fright
and then again
we're climbing

viii. Taft Pioneer Cemetery and Belden Creek Road

it's twenty twenty-four
how did you find this place
at the house
north of Corvallis
my brother's fingers
on the photo trace
the shape
of my daughter's face

Hunter Brook
Piper Cook

the curve of the waves
beneath the graves
my mother's gray hair
blown strange
and strayed

My father's past
grows halts
and gaps

Fennel Crop
Woody Sapp

needle threaded
through an eye
stitch cotton weave
extra ease

over cloth worn
to a sigh
a breath exhaled
into a cloud

Wolf Grove Funk
Tower Love Park

last year lost
last—
                a ghost
the recent past
fades quickly

but the stories
stored away from light
he takes them out
the colors bright

in nineteen forty-four
the Coast Guard
built a watchtower here
enabled a panoramic view
of any threats from the sea

the ocean
far below us
swallowing
her own
whitecaps

Sweet Grief
Hand Kraft

My brother asks *do you remember a book we read as*
children I'm sure you read it too some children get lost
and eventually arrive at a house where everything is powered
by backwards magic Our father says *letting the air out*
of a balloon won't make it go up! My brother says *Yes*
It is hard not to get frustrated when your father
is confused *It was magic everything was backwards* We
walked through a tunnel in order to climb a cliff
I don't remember it I say *but I believe that I read it*

in the photos my daughter
runs and runs
it's a patch
of bias-cut grass
and graves

creeping gromwell
surrounded by salal
overgrowing
the stone and chain
link fences

though parts
of the original
structure remain

the memorial is
not an exact
replica

bird's foot
trefoils
hunched in
yellow bunches
weedy and windy

Still Fell
Swallow Bell

we're at the most beautiful
cemetery in the world

My husband and I sit on a bench
looking out at the waves
I make my mouth into the shapes
of the names on the graves

Miller Key Catch
Chase Buck Watch

My parents, hand in hand
make small dark shapes
against the sun

Noble Young
Cherry Prong

When I write *back home*
there's no way to know
which way I was going

ix. Nona

sounds as threads
that baste together
living and dead
The House of
the Sewn Tongue

Grendel is always
in Druid Ridge

Grendel-yet-to-come
her memory or her ghost
or animal alive and deep
in the joy of the
smells of life and death
which are the same smells

Judge Archer
Leaf Badger

here's a game we call
cemetery section
or quilt block

Wye Oak
Pine Tree
Goose Pond
Economy

she pulls us to the edge
of the grass
between Hickory Knoll
and the lake
a complete deer skull
bone white
both antlers intact
stares back

The fates evolved over time
incalculable beings
agents of the divine
Now the lines are cast

you may ask
your question

A vast number of empirical studies support the health
benefits of green urban spaces however the number of studies
looking at the health benefits of cemeteries is sparse.

it's late summer
it's a backwards
magic laughing
as we carry bones found
in a burial ground home

Moody Huff
Dandy Duff

We place it
facing the sun
but under
the smoke tree
we're bone thieves

She made coffins for herself and other family members
and basted them in the border   when they died she moved
their coffins to the central graveyard

it's the end
of the empire
we churn out
grave goods for
the civilizations
of the Anthropocene
plastic knick-
knacks and single-
use packaging
are we
the baddies

I show my daughter
how to weave
a crown for
the skull
blanket flower

and black-eyed
susans in a braid
around the antlers
and over the
eye sockets

x. Alberton Road Hike to Ruins of Oella Mill and St. Stanislas Church

it's twenty
twenty-three
and when I
finally go back
to that particular path
after Atropos
unclipped my little
dog's lead I hear her
ghost scruffing around
in the underbrush

Consider straightening out the fibers of a cotton ball to make a long continuous stream

a heron
on a stone
in the river
leaps into the air
Return from the church
down the white gravel road
and turn right
sunlight hatched

on the graves flat
in the moss tuft

What remains
of dead you never knew
in the sunlight caught
on the sides of trees

Bald Ward Feete
Reed Beard Means

she'd bound up
the steep path to the ruins
a ghost community
a dead cemetery

what could be clearer
proof of life
than goose shit on the banks
the little holes
deer made with their hooves

This is the point at which hikers
must look carefully

along the hike visitors will see
an abandoned road
nobody could see
that road but
Grendel sniffed it out
and showed it to me
in a light snow
several abandoned vehicles
two abandoned churches

stones in place less than two
hundred years and it's already
a ruin

Brunt Mace
Flint Bass

trailhead near enough
to my daughter's school
we could steal time
stop by to unwind
or spool out a little
of the little dog's one wild
and precious life

How tedious would this be to make a shirt or even a sock
by slowly making each string by hand then weaving them
together into a cloth   Unless you took your time
how consistent would the thickness of your shirt be

I memorized the split
of a dead tree across
from the split
where the faded old road
spit-spliced into the new and
after that we often picked up
a short row
out and back
to the top of the track

please do not touch or damage the remaining gravestones

at five years old
my daughter made
joke salads *why*
did the pig become a firefighter
Because you have a pickle on your head!

It was twenty twenty-one
we drove past Druid
Ridge *what game*
do you play when
you are sleeping she asked
looking out at the
hills covered in graves
I don't know I say
she shouts it
dead!
I can't help it
I laugh

Olden Guard
Levy Ford

at home
the little dog
flopped on her back
paws paddling
the air as if to
pass a shuttle
through open shed

Foster Ray
Potter Quail

it's a strand of weft
picked and beat in
a memory of one
cemetery nested inside
a memory of another

old quilts may have been made
into batting
for a new quilt

xi. Mending

when cloth wears thin
a hole-sized mend
will rend the place you intend
                                                        ed
to repair

Sharp Glass
Sexton Mass

don't despair
or weep
in your chair
cut cloth to size
the width of your thigh
a panel can parallel
the old threadbare

Fewer Combs
Chasm Dooms

there
new fabric will care
for what's worn
and frayed

I don't know the dead here
but I've learned some
of their names

Emory Augur
Woodward Waters

xii. One of the Oldest Established Neighborhoods in Pikesville

It's twenty fifteen
and the baby is a girl
we tried out so many names
it's weird to choose a name
for another human my husband
says *and none of these sound*
great with Hurwitz
I look at him
surprised *Virgil*
does he says the names
together aloud

Barricks Lazarus Grimm
Marshall Dimmling Chin

These symbols   the spindle the swift
the needle the quilt
the names of the dead
the stuff you stitch
the things they said
the stuff you twine or twist
the tools you use

sounds wound around or cut
the chisel & pick
or thimble and thread
repair and the limits of repair
things that wear
away laid over things
that wear away

Woolwine Turner
Tailor Fray
Peel Lyon
Barber Shea

when we finally arrived
to our own drive in Ralston
I found a layer of leftover
pink raspberries shriveled
and shrunk
in their box in the trunk

tossed them out
in front of the house
for the birds to find
I didn't mind

Crane Perch
Weede Ditch

over time the name
I thought of as my husband's
sanding down into a name
I thought of as my daughter's
when I say it
I hear her wits
her wits it fits
she's clever
and swift

Fletcher Dell
Rider Fallin

My hand on the patch
pieced into the back
of the *Northern Lights*
quilt *the woman who is in*
a state of suspen
sion
dependent upon
the contingencies of history
that have formed her present
I don't know
anything about this cloth
except what color
it is now
cut out the word *cloth*
and stitch in the word *name*

Waldron Avenue was probably named
for the pastor of nearby St. Charles
Borromeo Church in Pikesville

lying down underneath
or inside patches
and patchwork names

laid on the ground
connected to other
names the way rook
is connected to knight

Dowell Heist
Short Mast

lives whittled down
to just a sound
or the space
those you left alive
believe you occupied
mother beloved wife
MY DARLING

Child Chestnut
Ashman King

xiii. Druid Ridge Cemetery

many a planner has toyed with the thought of all the good things that could be done with the land

never mind who was buried there
before Harrison built Annandale
before colonists landed
and landed themselves
granted themselves land
hands *plan ahead*
and save you too
can get a grave
in *Evergreen* or *Forest Lawn*

storytelling
gossip the exchange
of information singing
plus the sharing
of a meal

Cross and Crown
Big Dipper

is it a wake
or a bee

Long Beech Port
Bare Reach Fort

flat grave markers reflect the western sun
this one says *MY DARLING*
lying down underneath
or inside patches
and patchwork
sentimental motifs
and images such as birds
violets butterflies

which is the right
sign

Duke Fewer
Justice Boone

our lives
bobbins
on a lazy kate
intertwined
or
    a single skein
made of time

When I read a gravemarker that reminds me when life
gives us scraps make quilts *the sun breaks through*
and I break out in a grin

xiv. Druid Ridge Cemetery and St. Borromeo Cemetery

the words on the graves
come around again
insisting on continuity
between the living and the dead
it's morning
Stiff, thin, the soul
within the body's prison
the games at night
the soul takes flight
and then in death it's risen

Call Cherry
Chancellor

the little dog is with me
or her ghost is
Dogs are allowed
but should be kept on a leash
at Druid Ridge
she's sniffing around
Clotho's feet

Herd Early
Ride Jolly

The cemetery is somewhat hidden
We had lived just three streets away
for almost fifteen years
before we realized
it was tucked between
the Catholic church
and the Jewish day school
still accepting new burials

My daughter and I find it
it's late twenty twenty
and we're looking
for new outdoor activities

which is to say
Here you may somehow
stay a little in peace
while in the park you find
people who grill and
lots of talking
we're looking for
new cemeteries
on google maps
Interviewer: Do you think this is a park
Interviewee: Uh sort of

Forest Dyer Field
Bean Willow Cedar

it's closer than
the playground
down in
Sudbrook Park
where *the ghost of*
T Rowe Price
is playing air hockey

My daughter writes
Austin
spent 64 min
looking at skeletons
in her homework
then we walk

through the cemetery
where Jimmy McNulty's
tombstone lies cracked
on the ground to get
to the cemetery where
the geese stand around

Beer Hall
Show Call

xv. Mending

sounds that come
around again
are slim
stitches

Childe Leaver
Nettles Seaver

threaded through thought
pulling it taut

Bones Good
Moss Wood

xvi. Clotho Creating the Alphabet

in the morning the hill puts
the whole cemetery in shade
steam rises from grass
over the graves
it's hard to remember the names
there are so many of them

Rice Baker
Round Sheets

patchwork graves
a family plot
a plait
plaited names

to conserve these elements with conventional methods
might paradoxically weaken their meaning

a named plot:
Edgemont
Hemlock
Forest Lawn
a shared plot
a crazy plan
a crazy quilt

Pate Hull
May Pole

a plot is a lot
of land
maybe small
maybe a lot

a patch
is a thatch
of grass
maybe tall
or maybe thin
where the sod
is newly turned

Elder Alder
Summer Swarm

Clotho
spins out
a length of thread
but in her lap it turns
to a garland
and she's still holding
scissors

the Fates evolved over time
there weren't always three
and the jobs weren't always clearly
portioned out

it's late in twenty nineteen
my daughter plays
at graves
she is young
and the dead have
interesting names

we've got birdwatchers who come in on a regular
basis we've got people who walk here

Fountain Grain
Jewell Stone

it's a cold morning
frost in engraved
spaces
on grave markers
where letters were carved

sound shapes
laced with ice

xvii. Taft Pioneer Cemetery

at the top of the ridge
five trees with trunks
like the hatch marks
of parallel whipstitch

The state's legal definition of a pioneer cemetery is any burial place that contains the remains of one or more persons who died before February 14 1909

branches blown
from years grown
reaching east
in the high salt wind

Foot Fisher
Peeple Fryer

There's Mary
standing hands flat
gown
bowed out
stone made cloth

Converse Gardner
Butler Barter

below us
off the edge of the cliff
the gulls float
in air gusting
like swells on the ocean

actually it's a pretty
unremarkable cemetery
a patch of grass and graves
but it's a fact:
it has the most breath
taking view
of any cemetery you've ever seen.

Goldsmith Walker
Nutty Baker

My daughter
launching off a leg
straight as another

stitch or tick mark
arms like wings
eyes flown

Angle Parsley
Bang Price Peach

she might
take flight
there's backwards magic
tunneling to climb
running down to rise

Vest Singer
Day Drake

It's twenty twenty-four
I'm not into cemeteries
anymore not like I was when I was little
she's nine
but I'll still go with you
if you want me to

names
turned
to words

The graveyard at the center of the quilt contains the coffins
of those who have passed on while the edges of the quilt
contain more coffins labeled for living family members

her face
a cloth
her heart
a plot
her wits
a quilt

Fantom Bird
Woodyard Woad

Author's Note:

The poems in this manuscript quote from and are in conversation with many sources I am indebted to, including:

Berglund, Richard. "Druid Ridge Cemetery" *Dying to Tell Their Stories* (2017)

Biro, Sasha L. "The Quilt as Personal Object." in J. Kemling (Ed), *The Cultural Power of Personal Objects: Traditional Accounts and New Perspectives* (2021).

Bowra, C. M. "A Prayer to the Fates." *The Classical Quarterly* 8, no. 3/4 (1958): 231–40.

Doss, Erika. "Spontaneous memorials and contemporary modes of mourning in America." *Material Religion* 2, no. 3 (2006): 294-318.

Harvey, Thomas. "Sacred spaces, common places: The cemetery in the contemporary American city." *Geographical Review* 96, no. 2 (2006): 295-312.

Houck, Michael C. and M. J. Cody. *Wild in the City: Exploring The Intertwine: The Portland-Vancouver Region's Network of Parks, Trails, and Natural Areas*. OSU Press and The Audubon Society of Portland (2012).

Johnson, Sarah. "Taft Pioneer Cemetery: "A view to die for" (with photos)." *Lincoln County Leader* (February 19, 2017).

Maryland Department of Natural Resources. "Alberton Self-Guided Hike."

Michael, Coby. *The Poison Path Herbal: Baneful Herbs, Medicinal Nightshades, and Ritual Entheogens*. Simon and Schuster, (2021)

Minarek, Elsie Holmelund. *Little Bear*. Harper Collins (1985)

"Saint Charles Borromeo Cemetery Baltimore County, Maryland." *interment.net*

Ruark, J.C. "Dedication ceremony set for Taft Pioneer Cemetery." *Lincoln County Leader* (April 23, 2024).

Skår, Margrete, Helena Nordh, and Grete Swensen. "Green urban cemeteries: More than just parks." *Journal of Urbanism: International Research on Placemaking and Urban Sustainability* 11, no. 3 (2018): 362-382.

Zelinsky, Wilbur. "Unearthly delights: cemetery names and the map of the changing American afterworld." *Geographies of the Mind: Essays in Historical Geosophy* (1976): 171-95.

www.ingramcontent.com/pod-product-compliance
Lightning Source LLC
LaVergne TN
LVHW090539110826
845146LV00003B/1174